Sewing in the Montessori Classroom

A MONTESSORI PRACTICAL LIFE CURRICULUM FOR THE PRIMARY AGES

Aimee Fagan

Charlottesville, Virginia

Aimee Fagan
University Montessori School
1034 Reservoir Rd.
Charlottesville, VA 22903
www.montessoriworksblog.com
aimeefagan@gmail.com

Book Layout ©2013 BookDesignTemplates.com

Ordering Information:
Quantity sales. Special discounts are available on quantity purchases by corporations, associations, and others. For details, contact the "Special Sales Department" at the address above.

Sewing in the Montessori Classroom, Aimee Fagan. 1st ed.
ISBN 978-0692393925

Table of Contents

For Maddy and Imogen, the two girls that mean the most to me.

CHAPTER ONE

Sewing in the Montessori Classroom

MEANINGFUL WORK

The basis of a well-functioning and normalized Montessori class is found in practical life, and a strong practical life curriculum is rooted in meaningful real work.

> If a child does not set a table for a group of people who are really going to eat, if he does not have real brushes for cleaning, and real carpets to sweep whenever they are used, if he does not himself have to wash and dry dishes and glasses he will never attain any real ability.[1]

With these words in my mind, I looked at the practical life activities that I had available in my class. I found that many of the lessons and materials I was offering were lacking. They were not real, meaningful, and truly practical. I knew that I wanted activities that were culturally and socially relevant and appealing in my classroom, but what could those lessons be? Polishing is great, but how many children really see their parents polishing the silver place settings? Spooning, tonging, pouring, and the like are quickly mastered when the lessons remain isolated on the tray rather than incorporated into the classroom's daily functioning. What materials could we use that would both appeal to the three-year-old and stay as appealing and engaging until that child was six? For me, the answer was sewing.

This curriculum is for all children, girls and boys, ages two and a half to past six. Over my years of sewing with children, I have seen boys enjoy stitching and knitting with as much, and at times even more, enthusiasm than girls. Throughout this book I will constantly refer to "the child" and I will interchange she and he, but know that all of these activities are not only appropriate for both girls and boys, but also interesting, creative, and engaging.

---

[1] Montessori, Maria. *The Discovery of the Child* (New York: Ballantine, 1972), 92.

COORDINATION, CONCENTRATION, INDEPENDENCE, AND ORDER

Meaningful and real work ties directly into the main goals of the Montessori practical life curriculum: coordination, concentration, independence, and creating a sense of order. These aims are the underlying framework of the Montessori pedagogy. Without developing and strengthening these foundational qualities, the child will not be successful with the bank game, the moveable alphabet, etc. Essentially, the child will not be able to access and engage completely with the Montessori environment.

The child's coordination develops and is refined through the actual process of the work, whether it is cutting Play-Doh with scissors or cross-stitching Xs on gingham, the child is practicing new ways of using her hands. All of the lessons in this book are sequential, moving from simple, unstructured sewing to complicated finger knitting. The lessons progress so that the child is constantly challenging and building on her coordination, fine motor skills, and motor planning. As she moves through the curriculum, these skills are cultivated, and this transfers to her work across the classroom.

In the Montessori environment, purposeful and meaningful work more often produces deeper concentration and engagement than lessons that are just done for the sake of novelty. This deeper focus and attention helps the child along the path to normalization, meaning that the child independently choose work that satisfies her, shows engaged concentration while working, and is a functioning social member of the class. When the child is making something real, it draws her deeper into the work and the processes involved. It is exciting for her to think of and create her own projects, even if they are as simple as picking beads for necklaces. These lessons make that connection for the child. They give her the opportunity to plan and create, and therefore focus and concentrate. We observe this consistently in our class: Sewing work produces some of the most focused and engaged work in the area of practical life across the age spans.

These sewing lessons are isolated to help the child be both independent and successful. We want her to be able to tie a knot before she can sew a pillow and allow her the independence to decide how long she wants her necklace to be and what color embroidery floss to use.

> How does he achieve this independence? He does it by means of a continuous activity. How does he become free? By means of constant effort. . . . we know that development results from activity. The

environment must be rich in motives which lend interest to activity and invite the child to conduct his own experiences.[2]

We want the child to be successful, and to help that happen we scaffold tasks that may be a little beyond her current independent working level. If she can't quite tie the knot correctly, we want her to know how to ask for help, either from a teacher or a friend. But to see the joy in a child's eyes when she has finished a project of her own design and undertaking, that is the moment that takes your breath away. It is through this scaffolding and the building of independence that the child becomes self-sufficient in the practical life area. The confidence gained from making these choices and being given the independence to follow through with the choice expands and permeates the child's whole being.

The sense of order in the Montessori class is often defined as knowing how to start a work, do the work, and clean up the work. But it is all the little details between those steps that really challenge and push and ultimately reinforce and build a strong, well-developed sense of order. It is knowing how to organize your thoughts and choose a work, then plan and arrange your materials based upon those ideas, how to start a work, what to do next, and the countless steps that come between the start and the end of the actual lesson. Finally, it is also how to respect the materials and the classroom and making sure that the material is returned to the right place and is ready for the next child. In accordance with Montessori theory and pedagogy, all of these sewing lessons involve planning, thinking, choices, and the organization of ideas, materials, and movements.

Independence is developed as the child moves through the curriculum and masters the steps. The sense of order is reinforced through the lessons, the coordination is developed through the actual work, and the concentration lengthens and grows as a result of the work. It is this deep and connected practical life curriculum that helps the development of the peaceful, fulfilled, and normalized child.

---

[2] Montessori, Maria. *The Absorbent Mind* (New York: Henry Holt and Company, 1995), 84.

THE IMPORTANCE OF THE HAND

The hand is the brains connection to the world around us. In today's world, there is a great deal of concern about children's development of fine motor skills. As our culture moves to being greatly screen-based, we are struggling with how to help the children in our classes who have poor fine motor skills and motor planning. We have to engage children with materials that require fine movements and encourage them to use the mind and the hand simultaneously.

The sewing sequence presented in this book begins the day the child comes into the class. When the two-and-a-half or three-year-olds walks into our class, we immediately start the simple handwork of cutting Play-Doh and stringing beads. By bringing the youngest children into the sewing sequence early, we are allowing them time to develop and hone their fine motor movements, which they will build as the lessons become more refined and challenging. We continue to present and prepare materials and lessons that stretch the child's skills and offer her the chance to continue to practice and refine her motor planning and fine motor skills.

This is how the sewing curriculum encompasses everything that the child needs to be practicing in the practical life area of the classroom: coordination, concentration, independence, and a sense of order. It reinforces the foundational skills and readies the child for success in other areas of the classroom. It calls to the children and entices them to work, and this love of learning, working, and creating then connects and expands across all areas of the classroom.

CHAPTER TWO

Preparing the Environment

A prepared environment is the basis of a Montessori classroom or home. A ready environment allows the child to access the materials without assistance and interference. Since we are all approaching this goal with a different space, our outcomes and environments will vary, but at the core we all want an aesthetically pleasing, child-centered, accessible environment that maintains a logical and sequential set of materials.

SPACE AND SHELVES

There are many ways to present sewing materials in your class or home, so you need to decide what will work best in your situation. In our classroom, we have dedicated an one entire work-shelf to sewing materials, and so for our practical life area we have a total of three different work-shelves, but that is not necessary or an option in every situation. There are many workable possibilities: You may have to tinker and adapt as you see how your children interact with the materials.

If you are setting this area up in your home, you may be fine with one shelf in a bookcase with approximately four materials available. In a classroom of twenty or more children, you will find that you will need more space and a larger variety of materials.

GATHERING VS. SELF-CONTAINED

We made a fundamental shift in our sewing curriculum in the last year. When I attended the American Montessori Society Annual Conference in 2014 in Dallas, I went to an inspiring session on practical life by Elizabeth Norman and Joan Schuler, both from the Seton Montessori Institute. The main focus was on why we create self-contained works where we place everything the child needs right on the tray. Is that how our homes are set up? Rather than self-contained activities on trays, in our home we go around and gather the supplies we need for a project, so the same should be true in our class. We should present the child with the opportunity to gather the materials he needs. This is the first year that we have fully implemented the concept of gathering materials.

There are many benefits to allowing the child to gather the needed materials. Gathering allows the child to have not only ownership of his environment, but also of his work. It is an empowering way to set up your class, giving the child the choice of how he wants to create and manage his work. Gathering allows the child to be a constant problem solver. He asks himself, "What materials do I need for this work? Which button shall I sew?" This opens the door to creativity instead of constraining his work to the materials on the tray, or even the initial lesson. As long as the child is using the materials respectfully and productively, he is free to create and follow his interests.

A shelf prepared for gathering

In the past, we have always had two trays prepared with the needed sewing tools. The child still gathered a few materials, mostly just picking the fabric that corresponded with the activity he was going to complete, such as making a bracelet or sewing a pouch. Now, however, we have two empty trays and all the materials and tools the child may need available on the top two levels of the work-shelf, and then the child decides and gathers what he will use for any given sewing work. We still prepare fabric for certain activities (pillow making, cross-stitch), but we set it up in such a way that the child makes more choices in terms of both materials and tools. There is also access to unprepared materials that encourage free sewing and project design.

BASIC MATERIALS

Space: We have dedicated a full four-level work-shelf to our sewing curriculum. We have used smaller shelves as well, or sewing materials can be incorporated into the existing practical life or art area of the classroom. The aim is to have enough space to present a varied amount of sequential work that meets the needs of the children you work with.

Trays: You will need a variety of trays for either the gathering method or the self-contained setup. My personal preference is to use a variety of natural trays and baskets and to keep similar work on the same tray all year. The necklace work is always on the same tray, even as the difficulty of the beads increases. This gives the child the visual sense that these are all the same work, and it reinforces the visual sense of order in the environment.

Embroidery floss: This is our go-to thread. It is thick enough that it does not often knot accidentally, and it is heavy enough that the child can see his stitches.

Plastic embroidery bobbins: This is what we use to wrap all our thread around. You can do the same thing with thin cardboard, but I like the uniformity of using the bobbins.

Needle threaders: I love the sturdy threaders by LoRan. They make threading a needle an independent activity for even the youngest children. You can buy them through Montessori Services or Amazon.

Pincushions: We use these for needle threading. They are a must for keeping the needle steady while the child uses the needle threader. A fellow teacher made ours from an Internet tutorial. You can also use corks or commercial pincushions.

Magnet and small dish: I keep a magnet in a small dish to hold the needle threader and the needle. This is not necessary, but I like to use it as a visual check. I ask the children, "Are both the needle and needle threader on the magnet?" when they clean up.

Assortment of needles: You need to make sure that the eye is large enough for the large hook of the needle threader and that the needle is sharp enough to go through your chosen fabric, but not too sharp. We never use the plastic needles, as I find them to be frustrating. My favorite needles are 22 Chenille Sharps. We do start the year with needles that are blunt, but we move to sharper needles as the materials make it necessary. You may need to have dull and sharp needles out at the same time, depending on the skill levels of the children. If you have different needles out, it is important to show the child how to test to see if the needle will go through the fabric that they have selected (especially if they are sewing through two layers of felt) or to have a visual way the children can tell whether they have selected the blunt or sharp needle.

Fabric: We use many types of fabric, as you will see in the following lessons. The basics are felt, burlap, and basic cotton. We buy packs of large sheets of felt from Discount School Supply and burlap and cotton from local fabric stores. I prefer plain fabrics at the start of the year, and we add designed and patterned fabric as the year goes on.

Scissors: This is one of the most important items. It can be so frustrating to children not to be able to cut the thread because the scissors are of poor quality or have become dull. We have had good luck with Fiskers and Westcott. Also, be aware that they will become dull, and a once-great pair of scissors can quickly become a frustrating pair.

Buttons: It can be tasking, but you really need to be sure that a threaded needle can fit through all the holes in the buttons that you put out. We start the year ordering plastic buttons through Discount School Supply, and they have large holes, but later in the year we put out an assortment of various buttons, all of which can be sewn with the needles available. We often have an older child sit down with a threaded (but not knotted) needle and sort out which buttons will work for the sewing shelf.

Embroidery hoops: We have a mix of sizes and shapes. I think the plastic ones hold up better than the wooden, but we use both. I will often put a hoop in our opening and closing work at the beginning of the year.

Beads: So many beads! We use pony beads and perler beads for necklace work and then mixed beads for embellishing sewing.

UNFINISHED WORK

It is important to have an established system in place for pausing unfinished work. Since many of the lessons and projects take more time than a morning work cycle, or the child needs a break, it is important for him to know that there is a way to take a break and return to the work later or the next day. Again, this gives the child a sense of control and autonomy over his work.

Some ideas for places to keep unfinished work include the top of a shelf, a special basket, or a personal folder. The main considerations for unfinished work are:

- What do they do with the sewing tools?
  - o We have the child cut the needle off the thread and return all the tools to their storage places.
- Where do they keep the unfinished work?
  - o We have them place it on an empty space on the top of the sewing shelf.
- How do you know to whom the work belongs?
  - o Our children place their nametag on top of their work to mark it.
- How do you make sure they continue to work on it?
  - o We encourage them to return to the work each day.

SAFETY

Letting children use real tools mandates the consideration of safety, not only for the child using the materials, but also for everyone in the class. Here are our parameters for sewing work. Make sure that you establish your guidelines, that the children know what they are, and that the expectation is that the rules are followed at all times.

- Scissors are always carried on a tray or with the hand clasped tightly over the blades with the blades facing down and the handles pointing up.

- Needles are always carried while stuck into a pincushion. If the child needs help tying a knot, they should thread the needle, stick the needle in the pincushion, and then bring the whole pincushion to a teacher or older child who can tie a knot. The same applies if he has finished his sewing and needs help tying a knot to end the work. He should place the needle in the pincushion and bring the project and the pincushion to the teacher or older child.

CHAPTER THREE

Preliminary Lessons

These lessons are grouped as preliminary because they focus on developing the foundational skills the child will need to be successful in the sewing curriculum. In addition to reinforcing the basic work cycle, the main skills we are looking to develop at this time are finger strength and dexterity, scissor skills, and eye-hand coordination. If you have already established lessons similar to these in another area of the class, there is no need to move them to your sewing area or to create a duplicate lesson in the sewing area of your class.

Pulling Apart Burlap

Materials
- Burlap cut into small rectangles, about 1 x 3 inches (should be in a small basket on the shelf)
- A tray with a small empty basket

- A large basket on a shelf for collecting burlap pieces (can be the same one used to collect yarn snippings)

Presentation

1. Invite the child to the lesson. Take one piece of burlap from the basket and place it on the tray. Take the tray to the table.
2. Starting with one edge, use the dominant hand to start pulling threads off the edge of the burlap.
3. Place threads in the small empty basket on the tray.
4. Once the whole piece has been unraveled, take the small basket and empty it into the large collection basket on the shelf.
5. Invite the child to get a piece of burlap and try.

Aims

- Coordination, concentration, independence, and order
- Refining fine motor skills

Age: 2.5+

Snipping Yarn

Materials

- A baby food jar with a hole punched in the lid
- A ball of yarn

- A pair of scissors
- A tray with a small empty basket
- A large basket on a shelf for collecting the yarn snippings (can be the same one used to collect the bits of burlap)

Presentation

1. The ball of yarn should be inside the jar with the end of the yarn coming through the lid.
2. Invite the child to the lesson and take the tray to the table.
3. Grasp the end of the yarn with the subdominant hand.
4. Pull the end of the yarn to the edge of the tray.
5. Pick up the scissors with the dominant hand.
6. Cut the yarn into small pieces working from left to right, placing the snippings into the small basket on the tray. Show the child how to make the last cut right next to the side of the baby food jar, not the hole. That allows a short tail of yarn to remain showing through the hole.
7. Repeat.
8. Empty the small basket of snipping into the collection basket on the shelf.
9. Invite the child to try.

We roll small balls of yarn so a child can snip an entire ball of yarn. This makes a natural end to the work. The child is done when the yarn is gone.

Inevitably, the yarn tail will go through the hole. Show the child how to open the jar and thread it back through the hole in the lid.

Once we remove this work from the shelf, the yarn jar remains on the shelf as a yarn source, and children who want to repeat this lesson can gather the materials they need to recreate the work.

Extensions

- Use the gathered snippings in collage works
- Put the snippings out for birds to make nests with in the spring

Aims

- Coordination, concentration, independence, and order
- Scissor skills

Age: 2.5+

Tying Knots

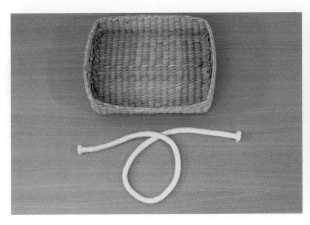 

Materials

- A piece of rope about 18 inches long (we like to start with heavy rope, and then move toward thinner materials)
- A basket to hold the rope

Presentation

1. Invite the child to the lesson. Take the basket to the table.
2. Lay the rope out flat.
3. Bring the two ends up and cross.
4. Take the tip of the rope on top and bring it down through the hole.
5. Pull tight to make a knot.
6. Invite the child to make as many knots as they like.
7. Demonstration how to untie the knots so the work is ready for the next person.

Extensions

- You can also use lengths of yarn, and the children can take the string home once they have tied it in knots.

Aims

- Coordination, concentration, independence, and order
- Preparation for tying thread in later sewing works

Age: 2.5+

Snipping Play-Doh

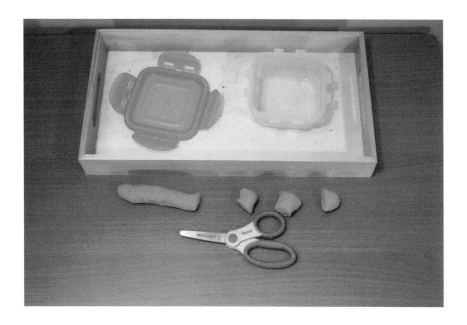

Materials
- An airtight container holding a small amount of Play-Doh
- A pair of scissors
- A tray holding the materials

Presentation
1. Invite the child to the lesson. Take the materials from the shelf to the table.
2. Remove the Play-Doh from the container.
3. Roll the Play-Doh into a long snake shape.
4. Use the scissors to snip the snake into pieces.
5. Collect the snippings and roll them back into a ball.
6. Return the Play-Doh to the container and replace the lid.
7. Invite the child to try.

Extensions
- Use an extruder to make a long snake. The extruder also helps to strengthen the hand.

Aims
- Coordination, concentration, independence, and order
- Hand strength and practice with cutting

Ages: 2.5+

Bead Stringing

Materials
- Beads with large holes
- A long shoelace with a plastic tip and either a bead or a large knot at the end
- A basket and tray to hold the materials

Presentation
1. Invite the child to the lesson. Take the materials from the shelf to either a table or a floor mat.
2. Remove the lace from the basket.
3. Demonstrate placing the plastic tip through the hole in the bead.
4. Slide the bead all the way to the end of the string.
5. Repeat for all beads.
6. Remove the beads from the string.
7. Invite the child to try.

Aims
- Coordination, concentration, independence, and order
- Practice for needle threading
- Later necklace/threading work

Age: 2.5+

Stringing Works That Make a Product

As the child moves through the early sewing lessons, a helpful way to encourage progress is to have her work with materials that create something tangible. This brings us to beading works that make a product. It starts simply, and all the following works are just a variation, or a progression in difficulty, on this initial lesson.

Pipe cleaner bead bracelets

Materials
- Pipe cleaners cut to a size that will fit a child's wrist
- An assortment of beads with large holes (we use pony beads)
- A container for the pipe cleaners
- A container for the beads
- A tray to hold the materials

Presentation
1. Invite the child to the lesson. Take the materials to the table.
2. Take a pipe cleaner.
3. Slide a bead onto the pipe cleaner, leaving about a half-inch at the bottom as a stopper.
4. Invite the child to add a bead.
5. Allow the child to bead the pipe cleaner, leaving about a half-inch of pipe cleaner at the top.

6. Twist the ends together to make a bracelet. The ends of the bracelet can be sharp: I try to bend the twisted ends to one side and slip a bead over the sharp ends.

Aims
*   Coordination, concentration, independence, and order
*   Practice fine motor skills
*   Prepare for later sewing work

Age: 2.5+

Necklace making

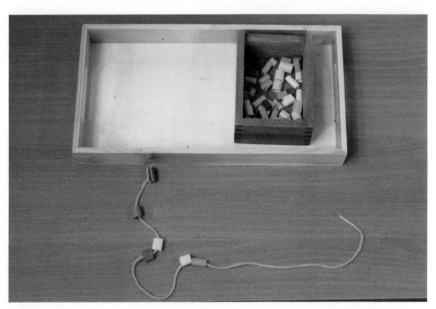

About a month into the school year, we introduce the necklace-making work into the sewing curriculum. We usually keep this work available throughout the whole year, keeping the tray setup the same, but increasing the difficulty of the actual beading material and slowly transitioning it to gathering work.

Materials
*   Yarn or thread in a container on the shelf (We start the year with premeasured yarn that has a bead tied to one end and a piece of tape at the other. By the end of the year, we have this set up as gathering work, the string is available on a spool, and the child cuts it as needed.)
*   A tray with a container of beads

Presentation
1. Invite the child to the lesson.
2. Show them how to take a string from the container and take the tray to the table.
3. Holding the string in the subdominant hand, use the dominant hand to add beads to the necklace.
4. Invite the child to continue beading the necklace.
5. Help the child to tie the necklace.

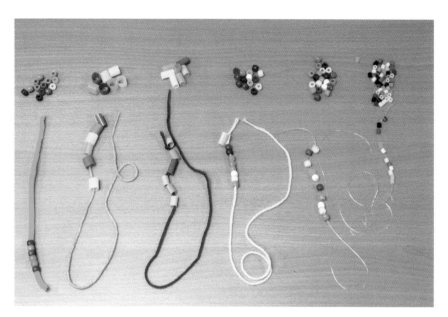

As the year goes on, we increase the difficulty of the materials.

We have necklace making available almost all year, but it increases in difficulty significantly from September to May. We gradually make the beads smaller and the thread thinner, and then we give the children independence in deciding how long to make their string. We generally follow this progression in difficulty for beading works:

- Bracelets with pipe cleaners
- Yarn (with tape at the tip and a stopper at the end) and large pasta or cut straws
- Prepared yarn and thinner straws
- Prepared yarn and pony beads
- Prepared elastic and pony beads
- Prepared elastic and smaller pony beads
- Prepared thinner elastic and perler beads
- A spool of thin elastic and mixed beads.

If using premeasured string, make sure that, when looped and tied, it is long enough to fit over the child's head.

We do not limit the amount of beads a child can use.

We do help the children tie their necklaces, but each time we do it we show them how to, as in a mini-lesson.

When and if you transition to just having elastic thread available, you will have to demonstrate how to tie a bead onto the end of the necklace to make a stopper. You may have to present this a few times or have some older children who can help tie beads.

Aims
- Coordination, concentration, independence, and order
- Practice fine motor skills
- Prepare for later sewing work

Age: 2.5+

Wire and beads

A final extension of beading work is to use wire and beads, allowing the children to create sculptures, mobiles, and other decorations.

Materials
- Precut wire of various lengths

- A collection of beads in a container
- A tray to hold the materials

Presentation

1. Invite the child to the lesson. Take the tray to the table.
2. Take one bead, move it to the end of the wire, and then twist the end up to make a stopper. You may need to show the child how to do this a few times before they have it.
3. Invite the child to add beads.
4. Help the child twist the last bead at the end.

Aims

- Coordination, concentration, independence, and order
- Practice fine motor skills
- Prepare for later sewing work

Age: 3.5+

CHAPTER FOUR

Early Sewing Lessons

As the child becomes proficient with the preliminary works, he can begin to move to the lessons categorized as early sewing. These materials, while still reinforcing many of the foundational skills from the preliminary lessons, begin to introduce new ideas into the curriculum: stitch practice, sewing vocabulary, and using the needle. There is no need to wait until the preliminary skills have been mastered to start presenting these lessons. Rather, the child can practice preliminary and early sewing lessons simultaneously.

Commercial Sewing Cards

Materials
- A sewing card
- A shoelace with a knot at one end
- A tray to hold the materials

Presentation
1. Invite the child to the lesson. Take the tray to the table.
2. Holding the sewing card in the subdominant hand, use the dominant hand to take the lace up from the bottom through a hole.
3. Move to the next hole and go down, demonstrating the running stitch. I find it helpful to use a repetitive saying, "Up from the bottom, pull, down from the top, pull," or just, "Up, pull, down, pull." This helps the child to stay on track and focuses his attention on which direction he is sewing.
4. Invite the child to try.
5. When complete, remove the lace from the sewing card.

"Up from the bottom, pull. Down from the top, pull" is my *running stitch mantra*. The simple phrase helps keep them focused on the next steps and reinforces the action.

You will help keep the children excited and interested in this work by rotating through a large selection of commercial sewing cards.

Aims
• Coordination, concentration, independence, and order
• Later sewing work
Age: 2.5+

Postcards or Cardboard Sewing Cards

Materials
- A container holding postcards or thin cardboard shapes (They should have holes punched around the edges and an attached piece of yarn with tape wrapped around the tip to start the sewing.)

Presentation
1. Invite the child to take a postcard from the basket. Take the material to the table.
2. Holding the card in the subdominant hand, use the dominant hand to go, "Up from the bottom, pull. Down from the top, pull," demonstrating a running stitch.
3. Invite the child to try.
4. The child can take the finished postcard home.

Extensions
- Children can use different colors of yarn to make patterns as they sew, such as a running stitch with red and a whipstitch with blue.
- As the year progresses, we just have the postcards punched with holes, and the child can independently cut the yarn and either tie it or tape it to the postcard.

Aims
- Coordination, concentration, independence, and order
- Preparation for later sewing work

- Stitch practice

Age: 2.5+

Stitch Practice: Running Stitch and Whipstitch

Materials
- Prepared strips that can be laminated and reused, or you can use vinyl (For the running stitch, have a long strip with holes down the middle. The whipstitch practice should use a rectangle that can be folded in half so the holes will match up on the sides.)
- A prethreaded needle with a bead attached as a stopper or a shoelace
- A tray to hold each stitch card

Presentation
1. Invite the child to the lesson. Take the tray to the table.
2. **Running stitch:** Holding the strip in the subdominant hand, take the needle or shoelace in the dominant hand and come up from the bottom, then down from the top. I say, "Up from the bottom, pull. Down from the top, pull," with each stitch I take. Finish the whole strip.
3. Say, "This is a running stitch. It runs all the way down the line."
4. Remove the stitches.
5. Invite the child to try.
6. **Whipstitch:** Fold the card or piece of vinyl in half so that the holes match up along the side.
7. Hold the card in the subdominant hand and take the needle or shoelace in the dominant hand. Come up from the bottom and go back around to the next hole on the bottom. I say, "Up from the bottom, pull, and back around." Continue until you have reached the end.
8. Say, "This is a whipstitch. See how it goes around the edge."

9. Remove the stitches.
10. Invite the child to try.

With the whipstitch I repeat the phrase, "Up from the bottom, pull, and go back around."

Extensions
- You can make individual stitch cards from construction paper, and the child can take them home when they have finished.

Aims
- Coordination, concentration, independence, and order
- Later sewing work
- Stitch practice

Age: 2.5+

Threading a Needle

 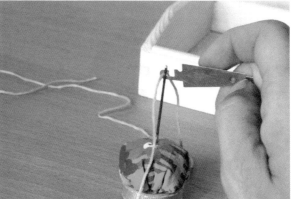

Many years we don't set this out as an individual work; we just incorporate it into the other early sewing works. Either way you choose to go, this basic-needle threading lesson remains the same. This is not a work I expect a child to master before he moves on to the next lessons, but we do continue to work and scaffold the task so it becomes an independent activity.

Materials
- A pincushion or cork
- A needle with a large eye
- A needle threader
- A precut length of thread

- A magnet (optional, to hold the needle and needle threader)
- A small dish for the magnet
- A tray to hold the materials

Presentation

1. Invite the child to the lesson. Take the tray to the table.
2. Holding the needle, point out the eye and name it. I say, "This is the eye. It's not like our eye, but it's the same word and even has a similar shape!"
3. Place the needle in the pincushion, showing that the eye is still upward.
4. Take the needle threader in the dominant hand and slide the large hook through the eye. Do not let go of the needle threader.
5. Pick up the thread with the subdominant hand and place it over the hook with about a two-inch tail at one end.
6. Hold the needle at the base with the subdominant hand. Using the dominant hand that is still holding the needle threader, pull the hook of the needle threader back through the eye until one end of the thread has come through the eye.
7. Point out that there is an end of the thread on each side of the eye.
8. Remove the thread.
9. Invite the child to try.

This is a hard task to master. Often with younger children, I place my hands over their hands as they guide the needle threader through the eye, and I help them keep it steady as they place the thread on the hook.

When the child is pulling the thread back out, the hook can get caught on the side of the needle, I try to show the child what has happened (Otherwise, they just keep pulling.), and then we push the needle threader back into the eye and try to remove it again.

We don't require perfect mastery of needle threading before the child moves on, but we do have them practice as often as possible and scaffold the lesson as needed.

Aims

- Coordination, concentration, independence, and order
- Preparation for later sewing work

Age: 3+

Tying a Knot for Sewing

For sewing with children in this age group, we do have them tie the ends of the thread together, so the needle will not come unthreaded. We have two ways to tie a knot, and both have their pros and cons. Practice both and see which works best for you. Usually we present both because some children prefer one way and others another. And still others come up with a different way!

Similar to threading a needle, this is not a lesson that we always put out as an individual work. Some school years the children enjoy practicing; other times the material is hardly touched. If we don't have it out as an isolated lesson, we present this same lesson as part of the initial sewing lessons.

Materials
- A pincushion or cork
- A needle with a large eye
- A needle threader
- Embroidery floss wrapped on a bobbin
- Scissors
- A magnet (optional, to hold the needle and needle threader)
- A small dish for the magnet
- A tray to hold the materials

Presentation I
1. Invite the child to the lesson. Take the materials to the table.
2. Measure the thread and cut. We use the measurement of the length of the table or the length of the child's arm. It ends up being about twenty inches. Based on your environment, you can adjust your method of measuring the thread.
3. Thread the needle as described in the previous lesson.
4. Remove the needle from the pincushion.
5. Bring the ends of the thread together so that they are even and the needle is in the middle of the thread.

6. In the dominant hand, pinch the ends on the thread.

7. Add the eye of the needle to the fingers that are pinching the end of the threads.

8. With the subdominant hand, grasp the floss in the middle.

9. With the subdominant hand, wrap the floss around the needle three times.
10. Now hold the tip of the needle with the subdominant hand.

11. Slide the dominant hand's pinched grip up to include the threads wrapped around the needle.
12. Holding the tip of the needle with the subdominant hand, slide the dominant hand (which is holding the wrapped thread, the eye of the needle, and the end of the thread) off the end of the needle and to the end of the thread.
13. If the child is going to start sewing, the needle is ready. If the lesson is finished, cut the knot off the needle and return the materials to the tray.

This lesson is the harder of the two options. It takes practice to make sure that you are pinching all the twists and the end of the thread. However, this method does produce the best knot. It is big enough that it doesn't accidently get pulled through the material, and it is always at the end of the thread.

This is one of the lessons that I usually do in an interactive fashion, rather than the traditional Montessori way of the teacher's presenting the whole lesson and then inviting the child. Because it is so complex, I find that children tend to master it faster if we do it together, and I use my hands to guide them, hand over hand.

Presentation II

1. Invite the child to the lesson. Take the materials to the table.
2. Measure the thread and cut. We use the measurement of the length of the table or the length of the child's arm. It ends up being about twenty inches. Based on your environment, you can adjust your method of measuring the thread.
3. Thread the needle as described in the previous lesson.
4. Remove the needle from the pincushion.
5. Bring the ends of the thread together so that they are even and the needle is in the middle of the thread.

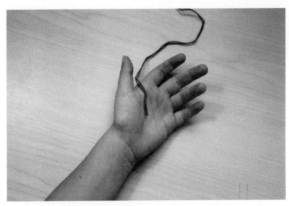

6. Lay the end of the thread in the palm of the subdominant hand.

7. Pinch down with the fingers to hold the thread, leaving the thumb sticking up.

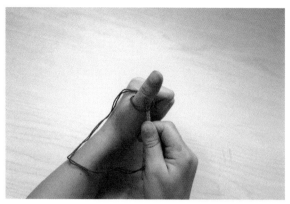

8. Grasping the needle, wrap the thread around the thumb.

9. Use the needle to sew under the thread.

10. Carefully remove the knot from the thumb.

11. Gently coax the loop down to the end of the thread

12. Pull the knot tight.

This is the easier method of tying a knot, but unfortunately the knot isn't very large and often the child tightens the knot in the middle of the thread and often cannot sew for very long without rethreading.

Aims

- Coordination, concentration, independence, and order
- Preparation for later sewing work
- Learning to tie a knot

Age: 3

Tapestry Table

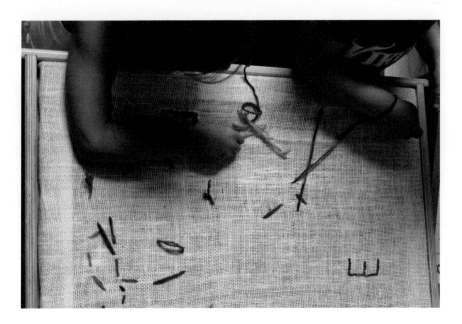

This is one of my favorite early sewing activities; it is one of the first lessons that bring together all the elements that the child has practiced. It is a stationary work, and we keep the prepared sewing tray tucked under the table when not in use. We try to keep our table out for most of the year.

Materials
- A tapestry table (It can be built inexpensively from coffee tables or small play train tables.)
- A dish with a magnet, a needle threader and a large-eyed needle (You have to be sure that the eye of the needle is large enough that a child can thread it with the yarn.)
- A pincushion
- A small ball of yarn
- A pair of scissors
- A tray to hold the materials (except the table)

Presentation
1. Invite the child to the lesson and have a seat next to the tapestry table.
2. Take the tray out from under the table and place it next to you.
3. Measure the yarn and cut. (We go as long as the tapestry table twice, all the way down and then back. Otherwise, they only have enough yarn to do a few stitches.)
4. Thread the needle and tie a knot as described in the previous lessons.
5. Sew on the burlap.

6. Cut the needle off and return the materials to the tray.

Aims

- Coordination, concentration, independence, and order
- Preparation for later sewing work

Age: 3+

Intermediate Sewing Lessons

The following activities are grouped as the intermediate lessons because with these lessons we start to implement the gathering aspect of our sewing shelf. In the beginning, we keeps thing very simple: the child only focuses on gathering the needed sewing tools, and there is only one choice of material. As the lessons progress, more materials, and therefore choices, are added. Restructuring your shelves to make them gathering-based is not a necessity. You can have trays prepared with the needed sewing tools, and then the child just collects the materials for the lesson she is going to work on.

However, switching your classroom to a gathering-based set-up for as many areas as possible is the most beneficial and empowering way to prepare the child's environment. For a more detailed explanation on the importance of gathering, please see page 5.

A gathering shelf, left to right: two empty trays, tray for scissors, two dishes with a needle and threader, tray of pin cushions, bowl of buttons, tray with thread and yarn. Second shelf, left to right: tray with shelf liner and plastic canvas, tray with burlap, tray with felt for bracelets, tray with felt for pouches, tray with cloth, embroidery hoop.

With the intermediate lessons, we aim to provide a variety of materials that continue to reinforce and develop the basic sewing skills. The lessons are not necessarily consecutive. Rather, they are parallel and present the child with different ways to practice the same skill set. As soon as the child is comfortable and somewhat independent with the beginning sewing lessons, she can start to practice these intermediate lessons.

We add these lessons to the shelf usually about six to eight weeks into the school year. This is usually when the class is beginning to settle into the routine and the newer children are comfortable with the basics of the classroom. Even though the class always has returning students who have previously worked on more advanced sewing lessons, it is important to start with the lessons at the beginning of this chapter. All the children need to review and remember the steps and the process of gathering and sewing. Every year we add lessons and materials in a different order, depending on the interest and the ability of the class. You have to observe your class and see what is needed and how the children are interacting with the materials available.

Sewing on Thick Material and Sewing a Knot to Finish

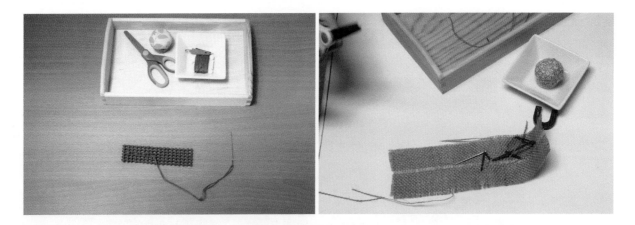

This is our first real sewing work. We usually start with shelf liner, and then switch to burlap, and finally have both available for the child to choose between. This is also when we start setting up the gathering nature of the sewing shelf. We spend a good deal of time focusing on gathering and preparing the sewing tray and then returning the materials for the next child, so we try to make these early lessons simple.

Materials
- A shelf set up for gathering materials
  - Trays
  - Scissors

> ○ Dishes with a needle, needle threader, and magnet
> ○ Collection of embroidery floss wrapped around bobbins
- Alternatively, a premade sewing tray that has all of these materials
- An assortment of burlap or shelf liner in a tray or basket

Presentation

1. Invite the child to the lesson.
2. Take them to the shelf and talk through your gathering: "I need a tray and a pair of scissors. What color thread should we use? I need my needle and threader and a piece of burlap."
3. If using burlap, show the child how to pull out and remove a few threads in the middle of the piece to make a line to sew on. You can also have the burlap prepared with lines drawn in marker, which I find helpful at the start of the year.
4. Invite the child to thread the needle and tie the knot; help as needed.
5. Holding the fabric in the subdominant hand, take the needle in the dominant hand and start from the bottom, coming through on the line. I always purposely miss the line the first time and show the child how to pull just the tip of the needle out and reposition it.
6. Before taking the next stitch, show the child to pull the needle until it stops. Then sew down from the top. We repeat, "Up from the bottom, pull. Down from the top, pull," as we sew, making sure to pull until the needle and thread stop.
7. Name the stitch. For example, "This is a running stitch. See how it runs right up the line."
8. You have two options now. You can invite the child to finish sewing the piece after you have done about two stitches, or you can easily undo your stitches and allow the child to start from the beginning.

9. This is when I first start showing a child how to finish their work. Making sure that the needle is on the back of the material, flip the whole piece over. Take the needle and sew back through the last stitch. Before you pull that tight, slip the needle through the loop

that has been created by the backstitching. Pull tight. Repeat. We call this "sewing a knot." Again, this is something that you will have to demonstrate and help with for quite a while.

10. When finished, return all the materials to the appropriate place so that everything is ready for the next child.

Prerequisites

- Lessons and practice on most of the preliminary and early sewing activities, especially those that practice the up/down pattern of the running stitch
- Work with the tapestry table

Aims

- Coordination, concentration, independence, and order
- Practice with the running stitch

Age: 3.5+

Sewing a Button onto Material

Materials

- A shelf set up for gathering or a prepared sewing tray
- A container with a selection of buttons (I find it helpful to start with buttons that just have two holes.)
- A tray with a collection of burlap or shelf liner cut into small squares

Presentation

1. Invite the child to the lesson.
2. Go to the shelf and gather the materials that you need, including the button and the fabric.
3. Have the child thread the needle and tie a knot, helping as needed.

4. Hold the fabric in the subdominant hand and take the needle in the dominant hand.

5. Hold the button on top of the fabric.

6. Come up through the fabric from the bottom and then through the hole in the button. I always demonstrate wiggling the needle around until the tip comes through the hole in the button.

7. Go back down through the opposite hole.

8. You have two options now. You can invite the child to finish sewing the button with two more stitches through the holes in the button, or you can undo your sewing and have the child start from the beginning. I usually undo my stitches and have them start from the beginning so they have the practice of finding that first hole.

9. To finish, show the child how to take the needle and sew underneath the previous stitches on the back of the fabric. Before they pull the loop tight, have them sew through the loop. This will be something that you will continue to present as they learn to tie a knot to finish. Repeat.

10. Return the materials to the shelf so that everything is ready for the next child.

Prerequisites
- Work with preliminary and early sewing work
- Sewing on burlap or shelf liner

Aims
- Coordination, concentration, independence, and order
- Practice with sewing a button

Age: 3.5+

Stitching on Plastic Canvas

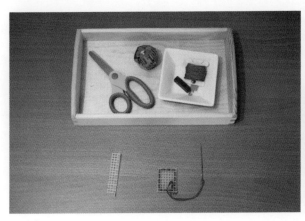 

Materials
- A shelf set up for gathering or a prepared sewing tray
- A container with plastic canvas cut into small rectangles

Presentation
1. Invite the child to the lesson.
2. Go to the shelf and gather the materials including the plastic canvas.
3. Have the child thread and knot the needle, helping and re-presenting the lesson if needed.
4. Holding the plastic canvas, point out the first long row on the dominant side. I say, "We are going to stitch all the way up this row."
5. Start at the bottom of the row and begin using a running stitch to sew up. Invite the child to take over.
6. When the child reaches the top of the row, show them how to start back down the next row or to go all the way around the edges of the canvas. The child can then sew as many rows as they like.
7. Return the materials to the shelf so that everything is ready for the next child.

I keep the canvas pieces rather small because there is nothing more disheartening than having too many rows for the child to complete.

Extensions
- The child then measures out a longer piece of floss and make a necklace with the canvas square.

Aims
- Coordination, concentration, independence, and order

- Practice with running stitch

Age: 3.5+

Button Bracelets

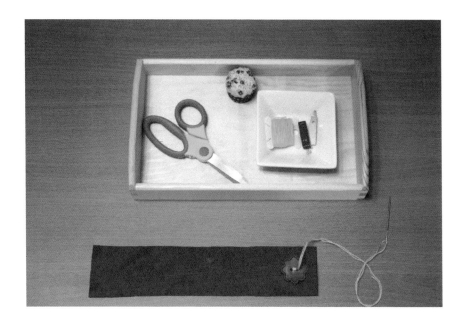

Materials
- A shelf set up for gathering or a prepared sewing tray
- A container of buttons
- A container of felt or flannel strips, about 2 x 9 inches each

Presentation
1. Invite the child to the lesson. Gather the materials and take them to the table.
2. Have the child thread the needle and tie a knot, helping as needed.
3. Holding the felt in the subdominant hand, place the button on top of the felt at one end of the strip.
4. Using the needle in the dominant hand, bring the needle through the bottom of the felt and through the button hole. I like to demonstrate missing the hole in the button at first, and then bringing the needle back out and trying again.
5. Show the child how to pull the needle and thread until it stops.
6. Sew down through the other hole.
7. Usually I try to take my stitch out and invite the child to start from the beginning.
8. We try to have them sew through the button three times to make sure that it is attached well.

9. Tie a knot on the back to finish.

10. Wrap the bracelet around the child's wrist, with the felt going over the button. Have the child pinch the felt where the button is, and then take the bracelet off.

11. Using the scissors, fold where the felt is pinched and make a little cut. I say, "We can always make the hole bigger, but we can't make it smaller." See if the button fits through the hole, and cut it bigger if needed. Again, this is something that you may have to demonstrate and help with a few times before the child is independent.

12. Return the materials to the shelf so that everything is ready for the next child.

We don't limit the amount of buttons a child can put on a bracelet, but we also don't advertise that they are all up for grabs.

Aims
- Coordination, concentration, independence, and order
- Sewing a button

Age: 3.5+

Felt Pocket

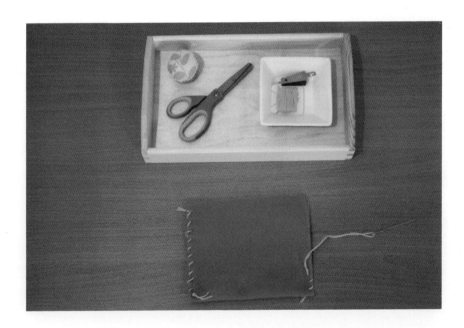

Materials
- A shelf set up for gathering or a prepared sewing tray
- A variety of felt sheets about 6 x 9 inches each in a basket

Presentation

1. Invite the child to the lesson. Gather the needed materials from the shelf and take them to your table.
2. Have the child thread the needle and tie a knot, helping as needed.
3. Take the piece of felt and fold it in half.
4. Holding the felt in the subdominant hand, show the child how to sew the sides together. I always demonstrate the whipstitch since it is the traditional stitch for joining two pieces of fabric. However, it does not matter which stitch the child uses.
5. Tie a knot at the end of the first side.
6. Rethread needle if needed.
7. Sew the other side closed.
8. Tie a knot.
9. Return the materials to the shelf so that everything is ready for the next child.

Aims

- Coordination, concentration, independence, and order
- Practice with attaching pieces of fabric

Age: 4+

Bookmarks

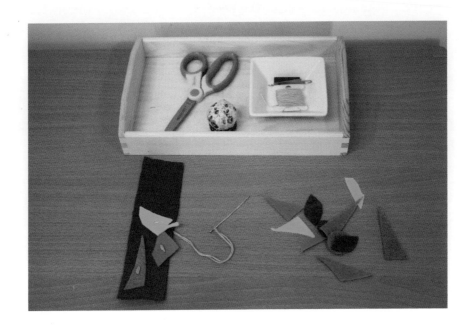

Materials
- A shelf set up for gathering or a prepared sewing tray
- Thin felt strips, about 2 x 9 inches each
- A collection of felt scraps

Presentation
1. Invite the child to the lesson. Gather the needed materials and take them to your table. Include a collection of felt scraps.
2. Have the child thread the needle and knot the thread, helping as needed.
3. Taking the felt strip and one felt scrap, place the scrap on top of the bookmark.
4. Show the child how to sew up from the bottom and through the scrap. Repeat so that there are two stitches in the scrap.
5. Invite the child to place the next piece of felt on the strip and sew up from the bottom through the scrap, making two stitches.
6. Repeat for all pieces of felt, rethreading needle as needed.
7. Tie knot.
8. Return the materials to the shelf so that everything is ready for the next child.

This is a lesson where it is easy to talk about the back and the front of the bookmark. I say, "I want my big stitches on the back, and my pieces of felt on the front."

Aims

- Coordination, concentration, independence, and order
- Practice with attaching materials
- Introduction to the front and back of a piece

Age: 4+

Stitching Prepared Shapes, Introducing a Hoop

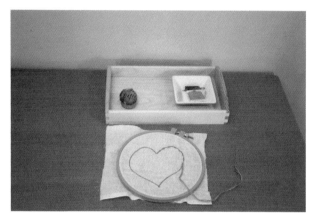 

Materials

- A shelf set up for gathering or a prepared sewing tray
- A collection of fabric (burlap or regular broadcloth) with basic shapes drawn on the pieces in marker
- A variety of embroidery hoops (I prefer the sturdy plastic ones.)

Presentation

1. Invite the child to the lesson. Gather the materials and take them to the table.
2. Have the child thread the needle and tie a knot, helping as needed.
3. Demonstrate how to open the embroidery hoop. Close it and invite the child to open it.
4. Lay the bottom hoop on the table and place the cloth on top. Push the second hoop over the top and tighten the hoops.
5. Hold the hoop in the subdominant hand and the needle in the dominant hand.
6. Sew up from the back, following the line of the shape. Invite the child to continue sewing.
7. Continue to sew along the line.
8. Tie a knot when finished.
9. Remove the embroidery hoop.
10. Return the materials to the shelf so that everything is ready for the next child.

Aims

- Coordination, concentration, independence, and order
- Introduction to the hoop
- Introduction to embroidery

Age: 4+

Embroidery - Drawing their Own Shapes

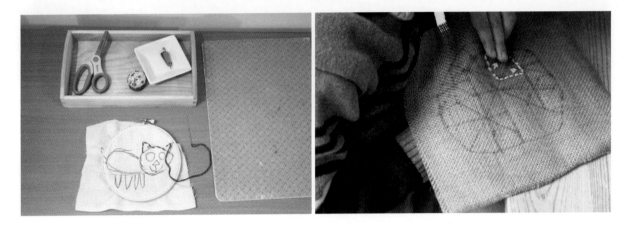

Materials

- A shelf set up for gathering or a prepared sewing tray
- One or two black markers and a corresponding number of placemats or art mats
- A variety of fabrics
- Embroidery hoops

Presentation I

1. Invite the child to the lesson. Gather the materials and take them to the table.
2. Place the fabric on top of the art mat.
3. Have the child pick a metal inset, continent, or some other item from the class and trace it onto the fabric. Have them return the item to its proper place.
4. Have the child thread the needle and tie the knot.
5. Sew along the drawn lines.
6. Tie a knot to finish the work.
7. Return the materials to the shelf so that everything is ready for the next child.

Presentation II

1. Invite the child to the lesson. Gather the materials and take them to the table.

2. Place the fabric on top of the art mat.
3. Invite the child to draw a picture of whatever they like.
4. Have the child thread the needle and tie the knot.
5. Sew along the drawn lines.
6. Tie a knot to finish the work.
7. Return the materials to the shelf so that everything is ready for the next child.

If the child draws a picture that is too large for the hoop, show her how to position most of it in the frame and then sew to the edge. Once she has reached the edge, show her how to reposition the hoop to finish her sewing.

Children will make far more complicated drawings than I could ever imagine. While we don't turn this into "drawing" work, they are free to make the picture however they would like it.

To keep the emphasis on sewing and not drawing, we only provide a thin-tipped black marker.

Aims
- Coordination, concentration, independence, and order
- Practice with embroidery

Age: 4+

Finger Puppets

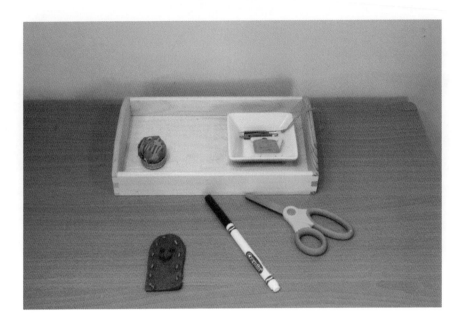

Materials
- A shelf set up for gathering or a prepared sewing tray
- Two pieces of felt, about 3 x 1.5 inches with a rounded top, pinned together with a safety pin.
- A thin black marker

Presentation
1. Invite the child to the lesson. Gather the materials and take them to the table.
2. Have the child thread the needle and tie a knot, helping as needed.
3. Point out that the child is going to sew from one side up and around to the other. Explain they will leave the bottom open for their finger.
4. Holding the felt in the subdominant hand and the needle in the dominant hand, begin sewing at the bottom of the puppet. I use a whipstitch, but the child can use the whipstitch or a running stitch.
5. Invite the child to take over.
6. Tie a knot at the end.
7. Use the marker to add eyes, mouth, or any other decorations.
8. Return the materials to the shelf so that everything is ready for the next child.

Aims
- Coordination, concentration, independence, and order

- Practice with joining two pieces of felt using whipstitch

Age: 4+

Pouches

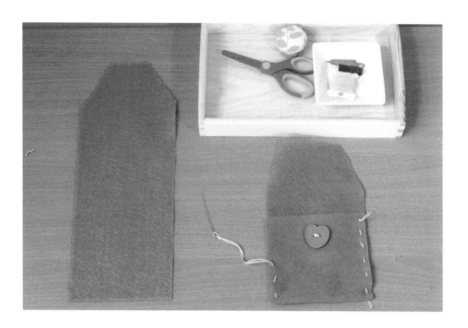

Materials
- A shelf set up for gathering or a prepared sewing tray
- A collection of buttons
- Felt sheets approximately 5 x 12 inches. You can angle the top edges in if you would like to

Presentation
1. Invite the child to the lesson. Gather the materials and take them to your table.
2. Have the child thread and knot the floss, helping as needed.
3. Take the piece of felt and position the button in the middle, close to the top.
4. Have the child attach the button, using about three stitches.
5. Tie off the button.
6. Have the child rethread the needle and tie knot.
7. Take the felt and fold it about two-thirds of the way back up, with the button on the outside lower area.
8. Sew one edge of the pouch closed and then tie a knot. I demonstrate with a whipstitch, but the child can use that or a running stitch.
9. Rethread the needle if needed.
10. Sew the other side of the pouch and tie a knot.

11. Fold the top flap down and cut a hole for the button.

12. Return the materials to the shelf so that everything is ready for the next child.

I often angle the top edges of the felt, especially when the work is new to the shelf. It is easier for the child to position the button and avoid sewing the flap to the pouch.

It is easy to add straps and make the pouch into a purse. To make straps, we have used pieces of yarn and finger knitting. Children have sewn together bracelet material, and they have cut their own straps from extra felt. The possibilities are endless.

Aims
- Coordination, concentration, independence, and order
- Practice with whipstitch
- Attaching a button

Age: 4.5+

Cross-stitching on Fabric

Materials
- A shelf set up for gathering or a prepared sewing tray
- Fabric with large squares (gingham)
- Embroidery hoops

Presentation
1. Invite the child to the lesson. Gather the needed materials and take them to the table.

2. Have the child thread the needle and tie a knot.
3. Place the fabric in the hoop.
4. Holding the hoop with the subdominant hand, take the needle and insert it at the bottom corner of one of the squares on the left-hand side.
5. Take the stitch to opposite corner, making a diagonal line like /.
6. Now insert the needle at the top left corner and take the stitch down to the lower right side, making an X.
7. Repeat in the next square or skip to the square of same color.
8. Tie a knot when done.
9. Return the materials to the shelf so that everything is ready for the next child.

Aims
*   Coordination, concentration, independence, and order
*   Practice with cross-stitch

Age: 4.5+

CHAPTER SIX

Advanced Sewing Lessons

The following lessons are categorized as advanced sewing lessons because the complexity of the lesson increases, as does the difficulty of the actual sewing. A child that is an advanced sewer is independent, a competent gatherer, and a planner. Such a child should be independent in threading the needle and tying knots and able to gather all materials needed for the projects.

Adding Beads to Embroidery

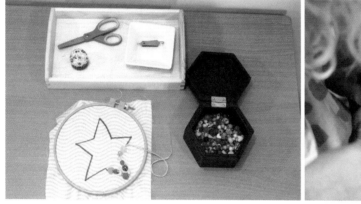 

Materials
- A shelf set up for gathering or a prepared sewing tray
- Embroidery hoops
- A variety of fabrics, either with drawn shapes or access to a marker and art mat
- A container of beads with holes large enough for the threaded needle to pass through

Presentation
1. Invite the child to the lesson. Gather the needed materials.
2. Have the child thread the needle and tie a knot.
3. Draw a picture or shape on the fabric.
4. Place the fabric in the hoop.

5. Begin sewing. When the needle is on the front side of the fabric, add a bead to the needle and sew back down to the backside of the fabric.

6. Invite the child to take over and continue adding one bead per stitch.

7. Tie a knot when done.

8. Return the materials to the shelf when done so that everything is ready for the next child.

This work is not actually harder than regular embroidery with a hoop, but we do wait until later in the year to add the beads. This adds a new element of interest and renews excitement in the work.

This can be coupled with embroidering on prepared shapes or with embroidery where the child has drawn pictures.

Aims
- Coordination, concentration, independence, and order
- Practice with embroidery

Age: 4.5+

Pillow Making

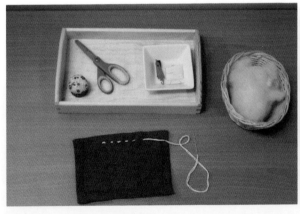 

Materials
- A shelf set up for gathering or a prepared sewing tray
- Precut felt in squares and circles safety-pinned together (This is to start. Once the work has been out for a while, we move to printed fabric with the "right" sides pinned together. Of course, we also have a collection of fabric and safety pins so children can design their own pillows.)
- A black marker

- A container holding fiber-fill stuffing

Presentation

1. Invite the child to the lesson. Take all the materials to the table.
2. Have the child thread the needle and tie a knot.
3. Using the marker, draw a line around the pillow, about a third of an inch from the edge. Do not connect the line. Leave a one-inch space between the two ends. This step is only necessary when a child is new to pillow sewing. Once they are used to the idea that they have to stop short so that they can stuff the pillow, it is no long needed.
4. Show the child to start at one end and sew along the line to the other end.
5. Once the child has reached the other end, they tie a knot.
6. Remove the safety pin and set to the side.
7. **Felt Pillow**: Fill the pillow with the stuffing
8. **Fabric Pillow**: Turn pillow right-side out by pushing it through the opening. The child will most likely need help with this the first few times. It can be helpful to have an orange stick or pencil to help to poke the corners out. Fill with stuffing.
9. Have the child rethread the needle and tie a knot.
10. Sew the pillow closed and tie a knot to finish.
11. Return the materials to the shelf so that everything is ready for the next child. Have a space to collect safety pins.

Children become very creative at this stage. We encourage children to draw shapes and make pillows that are doll-shaped, cat-shaped, etc.

Pillow making is easily combined with other sewing work. A child who has embroidered a continent shape on to fabric may want to make it into a pillow. Sometimes you may have to suggest these ideas first, but once the children know that the sewing shelf is open-ended, they will surprise you with their creativity.

Aims

- Coordination, concentration, independence, and order
- Sewing practice
- Making a product

Age: 4.5+

Free Sewing

Materials

- A shelf set up for gathering or a prepared sewing tray
- A variety of buttons, fabrics, yarns, and threads

Presentation

1. Usually a child comes to this on his own, combining lessons, mixing works, but occasionally a child might need a little encouragement. I find that the phrase "I wonder" is always a great starting point. For example, "I wonder what else you could do with that embroidery you just finished." "I wonder if there is a way to make a pillow with beads." "I wonder if you can make something totally new, that you've never seen before, with the materials on the sewing shelf."

Aims

- Coordination, concentration, independence, and order
- Sewing practice
- Making a product

Age: 4.5+

SEWING IN THE MONTESSORI CLASS | 59

Drawstring Bag

This is a great work, but it is one of the only lessons where the child does not tie the two loose ends of the thread together. It can become frustrating for the child who keeps unthreading his needle.

Materials
- A shelf set up for gathering or a prepared sewing tray
- Fabric cut into a circle with a diameter of at least ten inches

Presentation
1. Invite the child to the lesson. Take all the materials to the table.
2. Measure out a length of thread about thirty inches long, which is longer than usual.
3. Have the child thread the needle. Show him that he will not tie the ends together.
4. Use a pencil or marker to draw a line all around the edge of the circle, about a half-inch in from the edge.
5. Have the child start sewing, leaving a long tail of thread.
6. Continue to sew all the way around the circle.
7. After the child has finished, tie the two threads together.
8. Draw the threads together to make a bag.
9. Return the materials to the shelf so that everything is ready for the next child.

Aims

- Coordination, concentration, independence, and order
- Practical sewing skills
- Creating a product

Age: 5+

Finger Knitting–Multiple Fingers

When I give this lesson, I always use a story to help the child remember what to do when. The words I use will be in italics next to the step in the presentation.

Materials
- A ball of yarn tucked inside a basket with an open weave (Have the tail of the yarn coming through the open weave or a prepared baby food jar.)

Presentation
1. Invite the child to the lesson. Take the basket to the table.
2. Have the child turn his subdominant hand palm up, and tie a slipknot onto the child's thumb. I tie the nonworking end of the yarn to the child's thumb just for the first few passes of knitting. It does not have to be tied, but I find that it is more secure and the child tend less to use the wrong end of the yarn. Try it both ways, and see which works for you.
3. *You are a farmer, and you have some very silly sheep.*

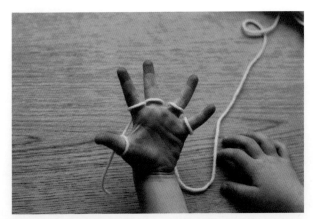

4. Take the yarn and wrap it under and around the index finger, then middle, then ring, and then pinkie. *These are your sheep. Do you know why they are so silly? They like to run away. They always jump over the fence.*

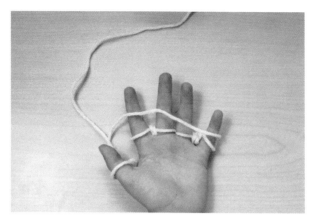

5. Take the yarn and lay it across the child's fingers above the "sheep." *This is the fence you build to keep your sheep back, but watch, they jump over the fence.*

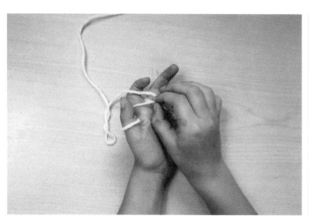 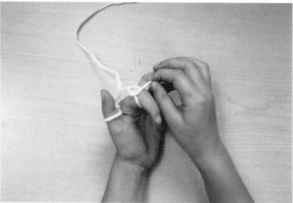

6. Take hold of the lower yarn and pull it up and over the "fence" yarn. Have the child curl his finger in a little. *And now this sheep jumps over the fence.* Repeat for all fingers.

7. Show the child that he is back to one set of loops on his fingers again. *There are your sheep!*

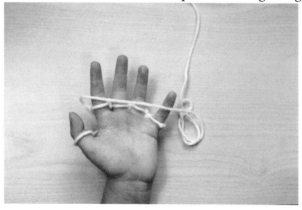

8. *Now we build a new fence.* Lay the string over the fingers, and repeat the process of "sheep jumping" by taking the lower string over the top string, each time saying *over the fence, over the fence.*

9. Once the child has made a few passes, you can remove the loops tied to the child's thumb.

10. Have the child knit to the desired length.

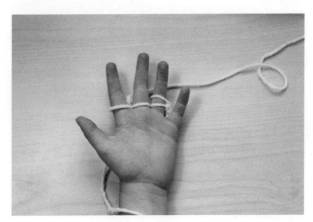

11. To cast off, *We are going to make the sheep disappear.* Have the child take the pinkie loop off and add it to the ring finger, bring the bottom loop over the top: *that sheep is gone!* Take the ring finger loop and put it on the middle finger, then take the bottom loop over the top. Next, take the middle finger loop to the index finger, and take the bottom loop over the top. Finally, cut the working end and bring it through the last loop and off the child's finger. Then tie the tail to the last loop.

Try to make sure that the child is always building the "fence" by just laying the yarn on top of their fingers. Often they end up wrapping it around the back of their hand. The knitting still works this way, but it uses more yarn and can cause more mistakes.

When starting, I tie the loose end to the child's thumb, because children often confuse the loose end and the working end when they first get started, and they knit with the wrong piece. I show them how to slip it off their thumb once they have made a few passes.

Even after children are proficient at finger knitting, they may still need help getting set up. We have them bring the basket to us, wherever we are, and we help get them get started.

Aims
*   Coordination, concentration, independence, and order
*   Preparation for other knitting crafts

Age: 5+

French Knitting

Materials
- A toilet paper tube with 4 or more Popsicle sticks taped securely to the side
- Scissors
- A yarn basket or baby food jar

Presentation
1. Invite the child to the lesson and take the materials to the table.
2. Thread the end of the yarn all the way through the tube so it peeks out of the bottom end of the tube.
3. Starting with the Popsicle stick at 12 o'clock, wrap the yarn around once in a clockwise direction.
4. Move to the stick at 9 o'clock and wrap in a clockwise direction.
5. Repeat for the 6 o'clock stick.
6. Do the same for the 3 o'clock stick. It should look like a square.

7. To knit, have the child place the yarn over the next stick on the *outside* of the tube, continuing to work counter-clockwise and then pull the bottom yarn over the top yarn and off the popsicle stick. It helps to have the child pull the bottom thread out a little bit and slide her thumb under to hold the top thread down while she lifts the top loop up and over the top of the Popsicle stick.

8. Continue in a counter-clockwise direction. (It is easy and natural for the child to hold the tube near her stomach and turn the tube as she works.)

9. To finish, cut the working end from the ball, thread the end under the loop, and then remove the loop from the stick. Repeat for all sticks.

10. To make it really secure, I then loop the end through the last loop that was removed and tie a knot.

When children first start, they will need help getting the knitting arranged. We help them for as long as they need it.

I still use the same story that I use for finger knitting. The first loop on the stick is the sheep and the child builds a fence, laying the yarn across the stick, above the first loop. But the sheep still runaway and jump over, and the child moves the lower loop over the top loop.

It takes a while for the knitting to become visible through the bottom on the tube. We have used a cardboard tube and Popsicle sticks cut shorter, and then wrapped tape along the bottom rough edges, that way the child has quicker feedback about the work.

Aims
- Coordination, concentration, independence, and order
- Preparation for other knitting crafts

Age: 5+

CHAPTER SEVEN

Sewing Projects

Throughout the school year, we are looking for opportunities to incorporate sewing into the culture of our class and school. We often have small projects going on in kindergarten, and for holidays we create a sewing project for the whole school that is accessible on all levels. Usually, these projects may require a little more assistance from an adult, such as using a glue gun, precutting some pieces of felt, or just being a little closer and offering more help as the project goes on.

We call these projects opposed to lessons since they are usually presented in a different way from materials on the sewing shelf, and often we work on them in a small group.

Peace Banner

Materials
- Dark blue felt squares
- White felt cut in the shape of a dove

- Needles and needle threader
- A dowel rod
- Embroidery floss (Metallic thread makes a lovely banner, but it can be very difficult to sew with.)
- Safety pins
- A white pencil or light fabric pencil
- A hot glue gun
- Ribbon

Process

1. Safety pin the dove onto the blue felt.
2. Have the children sew the dove onto the felt backing.
3. Adding the word *Peace* is optional. Often for younger children we just have them sew the dove. If desired, you can use the pencil to write the year or the word "Peace."
4. Have the children stitch along the writing. For older children, this is when we start introducing backstitch.
5. Have an adult cut the dowel so there is about a half-inch overhang on each side. A serrated knife usually works. If you have woodworking materials in your class, the children can cut the dowels.
6. Have an adult use the glue gun to attach the felt to the dowel, folding the felt over the dowel.
7. Tie ribbon to each end of the dowel.

This is how we teach backstitching. I gather a group of a few children, and I have a piece of the blue felt and some white floss. Using the white pencil, I write a capital P (I don't make it too large because I am going to sew the whole letter in front of the children.) for "Peace." I say, "I want to sew this letter P, but I want to make it so we don't see any of the white pencil. I want the P to be all white thread. I'm going to use something called the backstitch. It's called the backstitch because, rather than always sewing forward, I'm going to sew back!" I make one regular stitch, and then I insert the needle into the back of the felt and come up where I would usually start your next stitch. "Now, usually I would just sew forward, but not today! I'm going back." I sew back to the last stitch. As I continue to make stitches, every time I ask the children, "Which way am I going to sew?" They say, "Back!"

Herb-Filled Pillows

Materials

- Felt or cloth cut into squares
- A needle and needle threader
- Embroidery floss
- A safety pin
- Lavender and buckwheat mix (about three-fourths buckwheat and one-fourth dried lavender. You can also use rice.)
- A funnel

Process

1. Have the cloth pinned together with the right sides facing.
2. Have the children sew along the edge about a quarter-inch in, leaving a one-inch opening. I usually use a permanent market to make a dot showing them where to stop. For this pillow, they have to make small stitches to keep the filling from coming out.
3. Take the safety pin off and have the children turn the pillow the right way out.
4. Using the funnel, fill the pillow with the buckwheat-lavender mixture.
5. Have the children sew the opening closed, again, with small stitches.
6. Tie a secure knot.

When doing this project, I do sometimes ask if I can help, and I use a threaded needle to reinforce some stitches and close any gaps.

Earth Pillow

Materials

- Felt either with the continents traced or blank felt and a marker
- Sharp child scissors
- Two large, blue felt circles
- Safety pins, thread, a needle, and a needle threader
- Stuffing

Process

1. Have the child cut the continents out of the felt. Older children can easily do this as long as they have good scissors.
2. Pin the continents onto the blue felt circles.
3. Have the child sew and attach the continents.
4. Sew the two hemispheres together, leaving space to stuff the pillow.
5. Stuff the pillow and sew it closed.

Neck Warmer

Materials
- A piece of fleece about 10 x 22 inches (Check with each child that these will fit over each of their heads when folded in half.)
- A needle, needle threader, and thread
- Scissors

Process
1. Fold the piece of fleece in half.
2. Using a running stitch or whipstitch, have the children sew the two short ends together, making a large loop. The children may have to rethread the needle as they work. Be sure the knots are secure.
3. Tie a knot to finish.

Felt Flowers

Materials
- Felt and cloth cut into variously sized circles
- Buttons
- A needle, needle threader, and thread
- Scissors

Process
1. Choose a few variously sized felt and cloth circles.
2. Thread the needle and tie a knot at the end.
3. Starting with the largest, thread the fabric onto the needle.
4. Repeat for all of the pieces of material.
5. Sew through the first hole in the button.
6. Sew back down through the second hole in the button and then all of the pieces of material. Depending on how thick the stack of cloth is, the child may need help pushing the needle through all of the material.
7. Tie a knot.
8. You can attach a pinback to make this into a brooch.

Embroidered Tea Towels

Materials

- Kitchen towels, flour sack (IKEA sells a type called TEKLA for .79 cents. Prewash the towels and lightly iron them.)
- An embroidery hoop
- A needle, thread, and a needle threader
- Scissors
- A pincushion
- A pencil

Process

- Trace the child's hand onto the lower middle part of the towel.
- Attach the embroidery hoop.
- Have the child backstitch along the pencil line.
- When complete, we write the child's name and the year on the edge of the towel.

Embroidered Bibs/Onesies

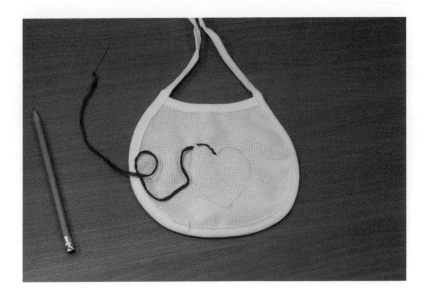

When we know that a child is going to become a big sibling, we invite that child to embroider a bib or an onesie for the new baby.

Materials
- Pre-washed cotton onesies or bibs
- A needle, needle threader, and thread
- Scissors
- An embroidery hoop
- A pencil

Process
1. Depending on the child's sewing ability, help them plan a design for the bib. Using the pencil, draw the design on the material.
2. Place the hoop around the design and have the child embroider the bib or onesie.
3. Tie a knot.

Bibs are easier for younger children because they don't have to worry about sewing into the back of the onesie.

Bibliography

Montessori, Maria. *The Absorbent Mind.* New York: Henry Holt and Company, 1995.

—————. *The Discovery of the Child.* New York: Ballantine, 1972.

ABOUT THE AUTHOR

Aimee Fagan has been working in Montessori since 2001. She completed her America Montessori Society Primary training at the Institute for Advanced Montessori Studies and earned her M.Ed. from the University of Virginia. Aimee lives in Charlottesville, Virginia, with her family. You can find her online at her blog Montessori Works, montessoriworksblog.com.

Printed in Poland
by Amazon Fulfillment
Poland Sp. z o.o., Wrocław